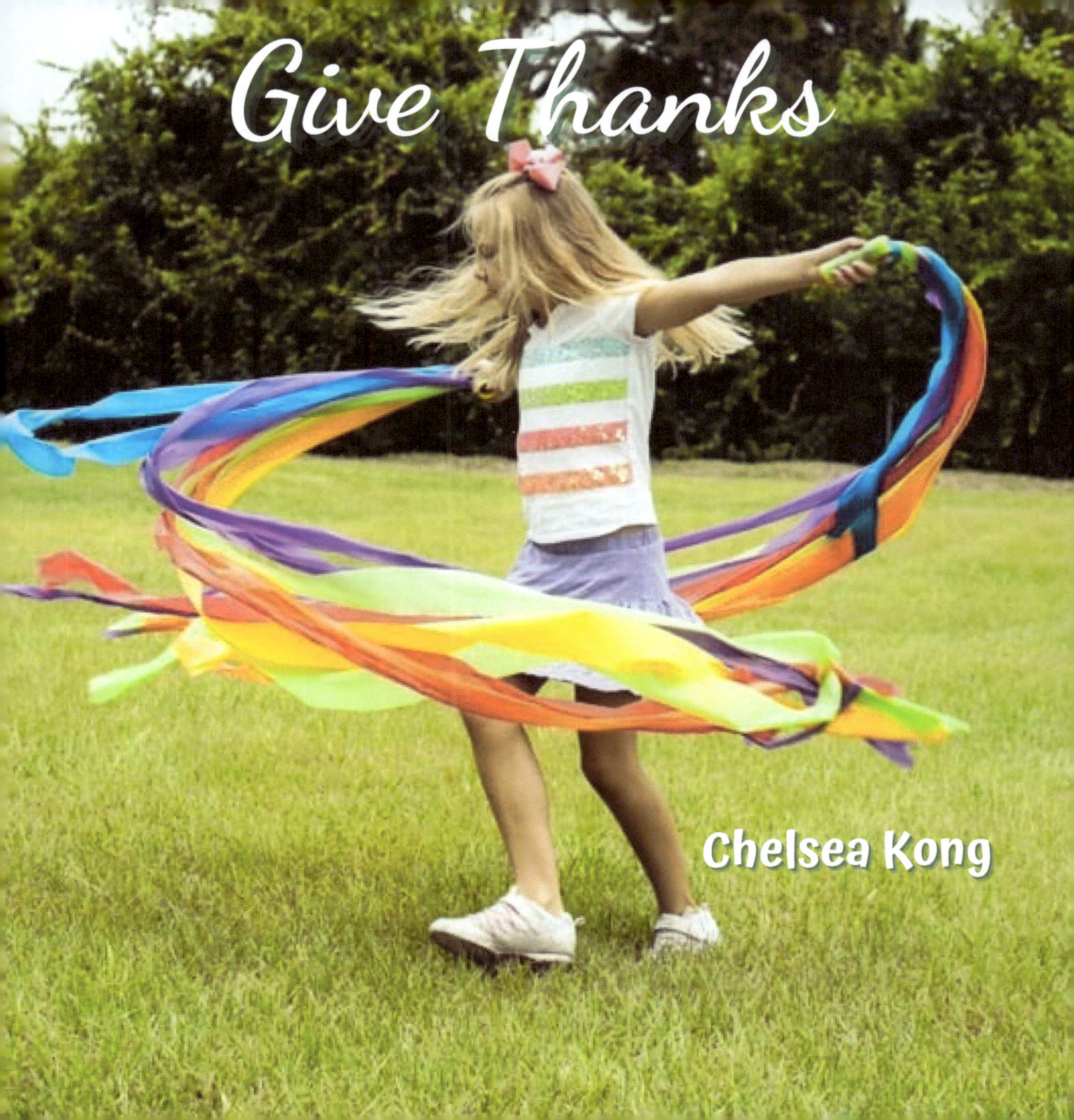

© 2023 Chelsea Kong

All rights reserved. All images used in this book are licensed copies from their respectful owners including Freepik, Pixabay, Pexels, Unsplash, Canva, etc. This book or any portion thereof may not be reproduced or used in any manner whatsoever without the express written permission of the publisher except for the use of brief quotations in a book review.

Printed in 2023, Made in Toronto, Canada
ISBN: 978-1-990399-23-7
Library and Archives Canada

GIVE THANKS AND REJOICE ALWAYS AT ALL TIMES.
{1 THESSALONIANS 5:18}
BE THANKFUL EVERY DAY.
A THANKFUL HEART BRINGS HEALING.

IT HAS POWER TO DESTROY THE DEVIL'S WORKS. WE GET VICTORY. {2 CORINTHIANS 2:14, 15:57} PRAY, BE WATCHFUL, AND GIVE THANKS {COLOSSIANS 4:2}

GOD LOVES IT WHEN WE GIVE THANKS.
HOLY SPIRIT WILL STAY WITH US.
IT BRINGS BLESSINGS.

IT MAKES US HAPPY AND OTHERS TOO.
IT GIVES US FAVOUR.
IT LETS US LIVE LONGER.

WE HAVE JOY AND GET GOOD SURPRISES.
IT BRINGS REWARDS. {RUTH 2:12}
WE ENJOY LIFE.

GIVE THANKS FOR THESE:
FAMILY, FRIENDS, HOME, AND CHURCH.
SCHOOL, WORK, FOOD, AND CLOTHES.

BLESS OTHERS AND YOU WILL BE BLESSED.
SAY THANK YOU TO OTHERS.
GIVE A GIFT TO SAY THANK YOU.

GIVE THANKS EVEN IN BAD TIMES.
THANK GOD FOR WHAT HE HAS DONE.
THANK GOD FOR WISDOM.

THANK HIM FOR THE GIFTS YOU HAVE.
THANK GOD FOR EVERYTHING.
NEVER STOP GIVING THANKS. {EPHESIANS 1:15–16}

THANKSGIVING MAKES THE DEVIL GO AWAY.
GIVE THANKS IN SONG, DANCE, PRAYER.
THANK JESUS FOR A NEW LIFE.

GOD KNOWS WHAT WE WANT. {PHILIPPIANS 4:6}
THANK GOD FOR HIS PROTECTION.
THANK GOD FOR OTHERS IN CHRIST.
{2 THESSALONIANS. 1:3}

PRAISE AND THANKSGIVING WITH A PURE HEART. {PSALM 50:14}

GIVE THANKS FOR GOD'S UNFAILING LOVE AND WONDERFUL DEEDS. {PSALM 107:8-9}

PRAISE WITH PSALMS, HYMNS, SONGS FROM THE SPIRIT. {EPHESIANS 19-20}
JESUS GAVE GOD PRAISE {MATT 11:25}

GIVE THANKS FOR WHO HE IS. {REVELATION 11:17}
GOD'S LOVE LASTS FOREVER {PSALM 107:1}
RIGHTEOUSNESS {PSALM 7:17}

MOST HIGH AND NAME. {PSALM 103:1-2, 106:2}
EXALT GOD'S NAME. {ISAIAH 25:1}
HE WILL ALSO EXALT YOUR NAME. {1 PETER 5:6}

WE MUST GIVE THANKS TO GOD.
PEACE MUST RULE. {COLOSSIANS 3:15}
COME BEFORE GOD WITH THANKSGIVING, MUSIC, AND SONG. {PSALM 15:2-3}

PRAYERS AND THANKSGIVING FOR ALL PEOPLE
{1 TIMOTHY 2:1}

WE MUST OVERFLOW IN THANKSGIVING. {COLOSSIANS 2:6-7, 2 CORINTHIANS 4:15-16}

SING AND BE GRATEFUL. {COLOSSIANS 3:16–17}
GOD SITS UPON THE PRAISES OF HIS PEOPLE.

GIVE THANKS THE LORD WITH YOUR HEART.
{PSALM 9:1}
ENTER HIS GATES WITH GIVE THANKSGIVING.
{PSALM 100:4}

GIVE THANKS TO THE LORD, GOD OF GODS, LORD OF LORDS. {PSALM 136:1-3}
HE IS OUR STRENGTH AND SHIELD. {PSALM 28:7}

SALVATION PRAYER

God, I know I sinned against you. Forgive me for the wrong that I have done. I believe that Jesus Christ died on the cross for me. That He rose from the grave so that after three days. I can have His long-lasting life. Come into my heart to be my Lord and Savior. I choose to turn away from my sins and I choose to follow you. Lead me to walk with you. Keep me safe and teach me your ways. Stop every bad thing in my life that has an open door to hurt me. Close those doors. Holy Spirit, fill me now in Jesus' name. Amen.

BAPTISM IN THE HOLY SPIRIT

Jesus, you are the one that fills me with Your Spirit. Come, Holy Spirit, and come into my life and fill me to overflow with Your presence. Come with your fire too. Thank you for the gift of tongues in Jesus' name. Amen.

Open your mouth and let the words come out that God gives you. It will be words you don't know what they mean. You can ask God what it means. You need to let Him talk through you every day to grow this gift.

He will bring you closer to God and you will know Jesus more. You will have power from God to do great things and know things.

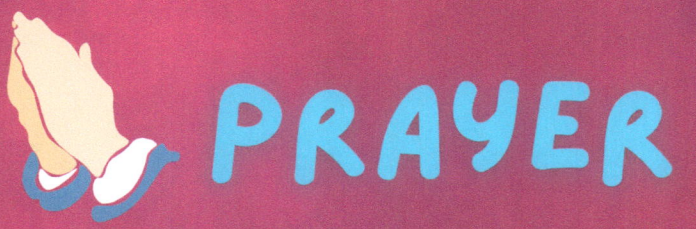

PRAYER

Thank you, Father, for dreams and visions. I pray you will give me the meaning of the dreams and visions that you give me. Teach me how to pray over them.

Guide my steps to walk in your ways and your plan safely in Jesus' name. Amen.

Message from the Author

God speaks to us through dreams when He can't get us to hear Him when we are awake. Dreams can also give us ideas. Visions can't change because God decides what He wants to do. We can also dream about heaven and hell. God brings people there so that they can share with others. He wants people to know Him. He wants them to have Jesus in their heart and the Holy Spirit to lead them. He wants us to put our trust in Him and tell Him everything. He will tell us what to do.

OTHER PRODUCTS

- Knowing God
- How to Hear God's Voice
- New Life in Jesus
- Loving Israel
- God's Gifts
- Meeting God
- Word Power
- Fruit of the Spirit
- The Tabernacle
- Bride for Jesus
- A Life of Prayer
- Live Free
- Who am I in Jesus
- Walk in Love
- God's Favor
- Man of God
- Woman of God
- How to Use Money
- God's Wisdom
- Fasting
- See Jerusalem and Bethany
- First Fruit Offering
- Feast of Trumpets
- Day of Atonement
- Feast of Tabernacles
- Counting the Omer
- Festival of Lights
- Glory, Presence, and Holy Spirit
- Live in God's Presence
- Pentecost
- See Galilee, Nazareth, and Tiberias
- 31 Day Devotional
- Biblical Puzzle Book Vol 1-5
- Bible Puzzles for Young Children Book 1-3
- Biblical Puzzle for Children Books 1-3
- Hear God Speak
- Knowing Jesus
- Knowing Holy Spirit
- A Health Life and Health Life Work Book
- Smokey the Cat
- Passover Unleavened Bread
- Resurrection Life
- The Blessing
- Chelsea's Psalms and Poems
- Revival
- Chelsea Learns Hebrew

OTHER PRODUCTS

Teaching Series
How to Hear God's Voice Teaching Guide & Audio Book
Relationship with God, Jesus, Holy Spirit Guide
Knowing God, Jesus, Holy Spirit Guide & Audio Book
Flowing in the Prophetic

Teaching (Non-Sale on the website)
Purim
Passover
Resurrection

More books to come!

More books on Amazon, Kobo, and Barnes and Noble, and Smashwords.
https://chelseak532002550.wordpress.com/

More books on Amazon, Kobo, and Barnes and Noble, and Smashwords
https://www.amazon.com/author/chelseakong

Please leave a review and share with friends to help the author continue to write more books to reach more readers.
Thank you so much for your support.

About
CHELSEA KONG

She is a writer, creative arts and digital media artist, skilled administration professional, and podcaster. Chelsea also served in a variety of roles, from audiovisual, photography, to assisting on the worship team, and ministry team. She also has a passion for families being united.

Chelsea has been a guest on Unity Live Radio, The Lady Tracey Show, and How to Live for Christ and is highly recommended by a Proud Christian blog. She is also a guest blogger. A few of her books have been featured in YourAuthorHub, etc. She graduated from Hotel and Restaurant Management, Digital Media Arts, Office Administration, Payroll Professional, and experience working with children. Chelsea lives in Toronto, Canada. She mainly writes children's books, stories, bridal writing, poems, lyrics for songs, words of encouragement, blessings, prayers, and jokes. The author of How to Hear the Voice of God, the Bridal Collection, Knowing God, etc. She also has her own Bible Puzzle books and other inspired products. Her podcast channel is called Chelsea K on Anchor, Spotify, and iTunes.

Please check my website to find out more:
https://chelseak532002550.wordpress.com/

www.ingramcontent.com/pod-product-compliance
Lightning Source LLC
Chambersburg PA
CBHW042055050526
44107CB00110B/1178